Read to Me

WRITTEN BY
Gill Davies

ILLUSTRATED BY
Angela Mills

Teddy in the Frost

When Teddy wakes up his neck hurts. His pillow must have fallen off the bed during the night and he has slept badly. Teddy does not want to get out of bed. He is in a bad mood!

"Time to get up, Teddy," calls his father. "Breakfast is ready."

Teddy grumbles and mumbles, then tumbles out of bed.

The sun is shining. Teddy goes straight up to the window. Outside the garden is white and sparkling. All the trees have silver edges.

Teddy's father comes to see if Teddy is awake.

"Look!" shouts Teddy. "It has been snowing!"

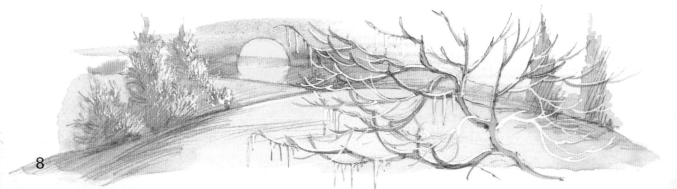

"That is not snow," says his father. "That is frost."

"It is snow, so there!" says Teddy crossly and he stamps his foot.

"You are in a bad mood," says his father. "Did you get out of bed the wrong side?"

"No," says Teddy, "I got out the same side that I usually get out of – but I lost my pillow."

Teddy goes downstairs. His breakfast is on the table.

"I do not like toast," says Teddy crossly.

"You are in a bad mood," says his mother. "Did you get out of bed the wrong side?"

"No," he says, "I got out the same side as usual but I lost my pillow and my neck hurts." Teddy eats the toast but he leaves all the crusts.

"We can put those crusts out for the birds," says Teddy's mother. "It is very cold out there today and the ground is hard, so it is difficult for the birds to find food. They will be very hungry."

"I know," says Teddy. "It has been snowing."

"That is not snow," says his mother. "That is frost."

"Well, it looks like snow," says Teddy and he bangs his spoon on the table.

"Do not be silly, Teddy!" says his mother. "You are in a bad mood today. Now put on your coat and go and take the crusts out to the garden for the birds."

Teddy puts on his coat and his boots.

Teddy goes outside. The frosty garden looks wonderful in the sunshine. There are icicles hanging like long shining fingers from the shed roof. A cobweb in the hedge has turned to glittering white lace and the grass sparkles. The pond is frozen, too. Teddy tips the toast crusts on to the bird table.

There are leaves under the trees that look as if they have been covered in sugar. They crackle and crunch under Teddy's boots. Suddenly Teddy feels very happy. His bad mood has gone. He scoops up an armful of the leaves and runs to show his mother and father how pretty they look.

Teddy is running very fast and he does not see how slippery the path is. There is some ice under the layer of frost. Suddenly Teddy slips. His feet slide on the slippery path. His legs fly up in the air and Teddy lands on his bottom!

Now Teddy has a sore bottom as well as a sore neck — and he has cut his paw. He begins to cry. His mother comes into the garden and picks Teddy up. She helps him into the house. Teddy's father comes to see if he is hurt.

"I'm not really crying," says Teddy as he wipes his eyes. "It's just that I am in a bad mood today. I think I got out of bed the wrong side – but it was the same side that I usually get out of – and I lost my pillow and my neck hurts. Now my bottom is sore and my paw is bleeding . . . but I am not crying, not really."

Teddy wipes his tears away. His mother puts a bandage on his paw and gives him a nice hot drink. Teddy feels better. He sits down and eats some more toast.

"I like toast," says Teddy and he eats every piece – even the crusts.

"Teddy, come quickly!" calls his mother. "Come and see what is happening."

The birds are eating the crusts that Teddy left on the bird table. Teddy watches the birds. He smiles and gives his mother a hug.

"I like birds," he says.

Then he looks at the white glittering garden and at the bandage on his paw.

"And I like frost, too," says Teddy. "Even if it does trip me up!"

Say these words again

pillow	table
breakfast	toast
shining	difficult
sparkling	mood
frost	fingers
crossly	frozen

What can you see?

coat

boots

cobweb

leaves

birds

Daisy Bear at the Farm

Daisy Bear has a toy farm with cows and sheep and pigs and hens and turkeys and ducks and geese. There are tractors and fences and little green trees and hedges. Daisy Bear lies on her tummy on the carpet and plays with the farm for hours and hours.

"It is absolutely my best toy," she says.

37

"One day," Daisy Bear says, "I should like to visit a real farm to see real cows and sheep and pigs and hens and turkeys and ducks and geese and tractors and fences and little green hedges and trees."

"That would be nice," says Mother.

"We shall see what we can do," says Father.

"Please can we go to the farm now?" asks Daisy Bear.

"No," says her father. "It is dark."

"No," says her mother. "You are a silly bear!"

"When can we go then?" asks Daisy Bear. "I am really looking forward to it!"

Daisy's mother gives her a hug and says, "We will take you to the farm tomorrow."

"Oh, thank you!" says Daisy Bear. She kisses her father, then she kisses her mother. "I wish it was tomorrow already."

That night, after Daisy Bear's mother has tucked her up in bed, Daisy falls asleep dreaming about her visit to the farm.

43

The next day the Bear family go to the farm.

Daisy Bear is very excited. She talks all the time and skips and jumps and runs as they go along Buttercup Lane to the farm on the hill.

"You are noisy today," says Mother.

"I always talk a lot when I am happy," says Daisy Bear.

Suddenly they come around a very big bend in Buttercup Lane, there before them is Hilltop Farm. "Look," says Daisy Bear. "I can see cows and sheep and pigs and hens and turkeys and ducks and geese. And there are tractors and fences and little green trees and hedges – just like my farm!"

"Welcome to Hilltop Farm," says Mrs Jones, coming out of the front door. "What would you like to see first, Daisy Bear?"
"I cannot decide what I would like to see first," says Daisy.
Mrs Jones laughs. "Let us start with the cows," she says.

"Hello, cows," says Daisy Bear.
"Moo," say the cows.
"Moo to you, too," says Daisy Bear. "I like you, cows. You are bigger than I thought but you have big, soft, kind eyes and beautiful, long eyelashes."
"Moo," reply the cows.

51

Next Daisy Bear talks to the sheep.

"Hello, sheep," says Daisy Bear.

"Baa," say the sheep.

"Baa to you, too," says Daisy Bear. "I like you, sheep. Your wool is harder and yellower than I thought, but you have such dear little faces."

"Baa," reply the sheep.

Next Daisy Bear talks to the pigs.
"Hello, pigs," says Daisy Bear.
"Oink-oink," say the pigs.
"Oink-oink to you, too," says
Daisy Bear. "I like you, pigs. You
are even fatter than I thought,
but you have sweet, little, curly
tails and floppy ears."
"Oink-oink," reply the pigs.

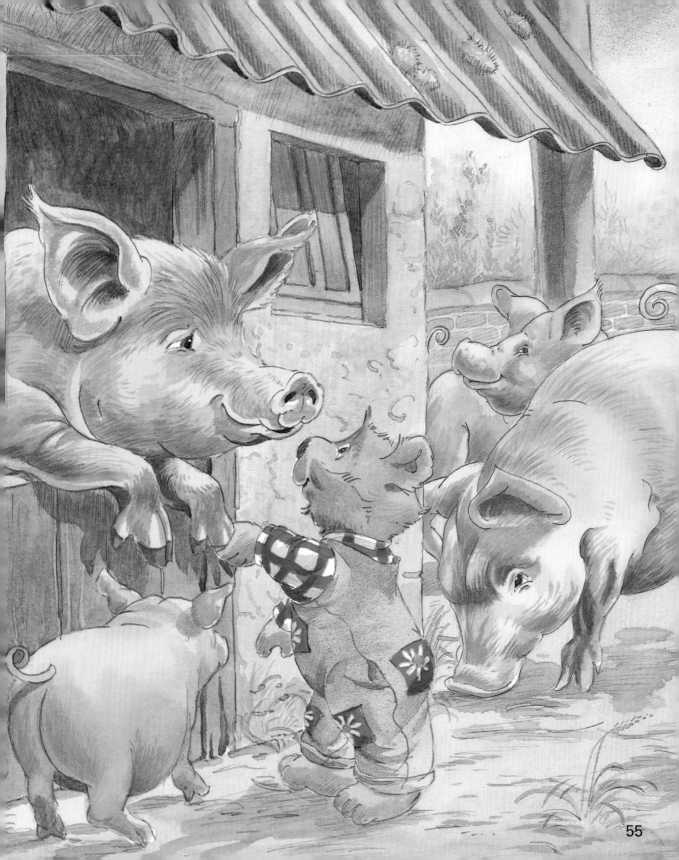

Next Daisy Bear talks to the hens and turkeys.

"Hello, hens and turkeys," says Daisy Bear.

"Cluck-cluck, gobble-gobble," say the hens and turkeys.

"Cluck-cluck, gobble-gobble to you, too," says Daisy Bear. "I like you, hens and turkeys. You make a lovely noise."

"Cluck-cluck, gobble-gobble," reply the hens and turkeys.

Next, Daisy Bear talks to the ducks and geese.

"Hello, ducks and geese," says Daisy Bear.

"Quack-quack," say the ducks, but the geese just hiss.

"Quack-quack to you, too," says Daisy Bear. "I like you, ducks, but I do not like the geese, they hiss and that is rude."

"Quack-quack," the ducks reply, but the geese just hiss.

Daisy Bear thanks Mrs Jones and goes home with her parents. At home she lies on the carpet and plays with her toy farm.

"It is absolutely my best toy," says Daisy Bear. "But one day, when I am grown up, I will have a REAL farm like Mrs Jones."

"That will be nice," says Mother.

"But I will not have any geese," says Daisy Bear, "because they hissed and were rude to me."

Say these words again.

carpet	tummy
little	farm
silly	tomorrow
kisses	dreaming
jumps	skips
decide	beautiful

What can you see?

cows

sheep

ducks and geese

hens and turkeys

pigs

Teddy Snowman

Teddy wants to be a snowman. "If I were a snowman," he says to the other toys in the bedroom, "all the children would come and dance round me and tell all their friends what a fine fellow I am. They would give me a woolly scarf to wear and a carrot for my nose."

Teddy goes over to the mirror and looks at his little black button nose. It is a very sweet little nose but Teddy does not like it.

"I do not like the little black button nose I have at the moment," says Teddy. "It is far too small. Snowmen have noses worth noticing!"

So, one cold Winter afternoon Teddy steps outside. It is snowing and the garden is all white. He has found a bright stripey scarf to wear. In one paw Teddy is holding a walking stick. In the other paw he is carrying a large carrot and some sticky tape.

Teddy stands in the middle of the garden and catches the snow in his paws.

"I do like snow," he says to a robin. "Snow is fun!"

Teddy fixes the carrot to his nose with the sticky tape. He stands very still. Teddy pretends to be a real snowman.

The children will see him soon and come out to play. Teddy is very happy. He can hardly wait to see the children's faces when they find him there. But nobody comes out. The children are inside watching the television. They cannot see Teddy Snowman standing outside in the garden.

Scrap the puppy from next door comes through the hedge and barks at Teddy.

"Woof! Woof!" says Scrap, running round Teddy and pouncing on his feet.

"Do not do that," says Teddy Snowman. "When you bark, I feel nervous. When I am nervous, I wobble. And if I wobble my nose will drop off!"

But Scrap the puppy is not
listening to Teddy any more.
He has found a bone and is
taking it back to his own
garden to bury it in the snow.
Teddy Snowman is sad that
Scrap does not want to stop
and play. Nor has Scrap
remembered to tell Teddy what
a fine nose he has.

Sukie the black cat is very surprised to see Teddy Snowman standing in the garden. "Purr, purr!" says Sukie, weaving round Teddy's legs. "Do not do that," says Teddy Snowman. "It tickles. If I am tickled, I wobble. If I wobble my nose will drop off!"

But Sukie the black cat is not listening to Teddy any more. She is chasing a sudden flurry of snowflakes up the garden path. Teddy is sad that Sukie does not want to stop and play. Nor has Sukie remembered to tell Teddy what a fine nose he has.

83

It is snowing harder now and
Teddy begins to shiver. The
sticky tape is now too wet to
stick properly and Teddy's
fine carrot nose tumbles down
into the snow.
It is getting dark.
The sun has painted the sky
a deep rosy pink behind the
trees.

Soon, it is supper time. Teddy is hungry. He picks up the carrot from the snow and eats it. Just then the door of the house opens for a moment. "Sukie! Sukie! Come in now," calls the children's mother.

Teddy can smell hot toast and butter.

"I think," says Teddy Snowman, "that I am going to pretend to melt!"

So he picks up his walking stick and marches along the snowy path behind Sukie. The robin hops down and pecks at the carrot crumbs that Teddy Snowman has left behind on the grass.

Teddy is indoors now in the warm house.

"Was it fun being a snowman?"
asks Daisy Doll.
"It was all right," says
Teddy, "but it is much warmer
being me – and I would not
want to eat my nose every day
for supper. Buttered toast is
nicer, especially with honey!"
Teddy Snowman smiles happily
as he licks a blob of honey
off the end of his little
black button nose.

91

Say these words again

bedroom	nobody
dance	barks
carrot	nervous
scarf	wobble
real	tickles
outside	snowflakes

Who can you see?

Robin

Teddy

Sukie

Scrap

Daisy Doll